SCALES FOR ADVANCED VIOLISTS

Violin by Johannes Franciscus Pressenda, Turin, 1823
Photos by Justin Robertson
Robertson & Sons Violin Shop Inc. Albuquerque, NM

© 2005
Preludio Music Inc.
Albuquerque, NM

ISBN 0-7579-4169-9

Preludio Music Inc.
exclusively distributed by
Alfred Music
PO Box 10003
Van Nuys, CA 91410-0003

lfred

Preludio
Music Inc.

Circle of 5ths

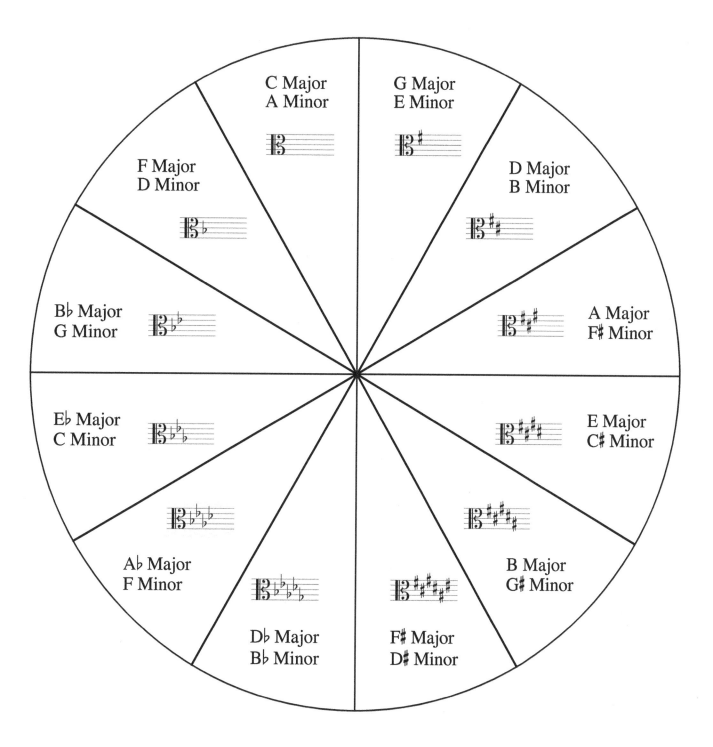

Chord Functions in the Key of C

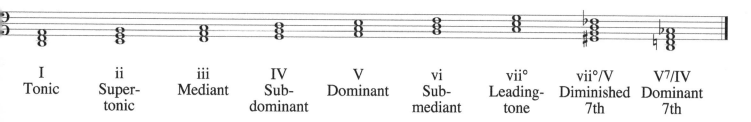

I	ii	iii	IV	V	vi	vii°	vii°/V	V7/IV
Tonic	Super-tonic	Mediant	Sub-dominant	Dominant	Sub-mediant	Leading-tone	Diminished 7th	Dominant 7th

Practice Suggestions for Scales and Arpeggios

The practice of scales need never be monotonous! Bowings and rhythms may be combined in dozens of different way in the practice of scales and arpeggios. The bowings and rhythmic variants shown here may be applied to the fa passage work in the violist's repertoire to develop and improve evenness, clarity, agility, speed and intonation. Only few basic bowings and rhythms are suggested here. The more notes played in one bow, the faster the tempo must b but never at the expense of accurate intonation. Imaginative combinations of these examples starting on bo down-bow and up-bow will produce endless variety.

The scales and seven arpeggio routine found in this book are based on the violin scale systems of Otokar Sevcik ar Carl Flesch and are adapted here for viola. The upper fingerings in the scales have been passed down through sever generations of teachers and students from the famous Belgian violinist, Eugène Ysaÿe. In Ysaÿe's system, the bo crosses the strings first, then the left hand shifts on the highest string. To avoid crossing strings on the 1/2 step for viol the lower fingerings begin on 1st finger. In the last five keys, a third fingering begins on the G string instead of the Violists may wish to circle their preferred fingerings to avoid confusion. So that the bow arm leads smoothly to the ne string, open strings are usually used on the ascending scale and fourth fingers on the descending. There are numero ways to play scales, arpeggios and double-stops, however, and teachers and students should feel free to employ variou fingering systems. Each practice suggestion is shown in the key of C and should be transposed into all keys.

Scales

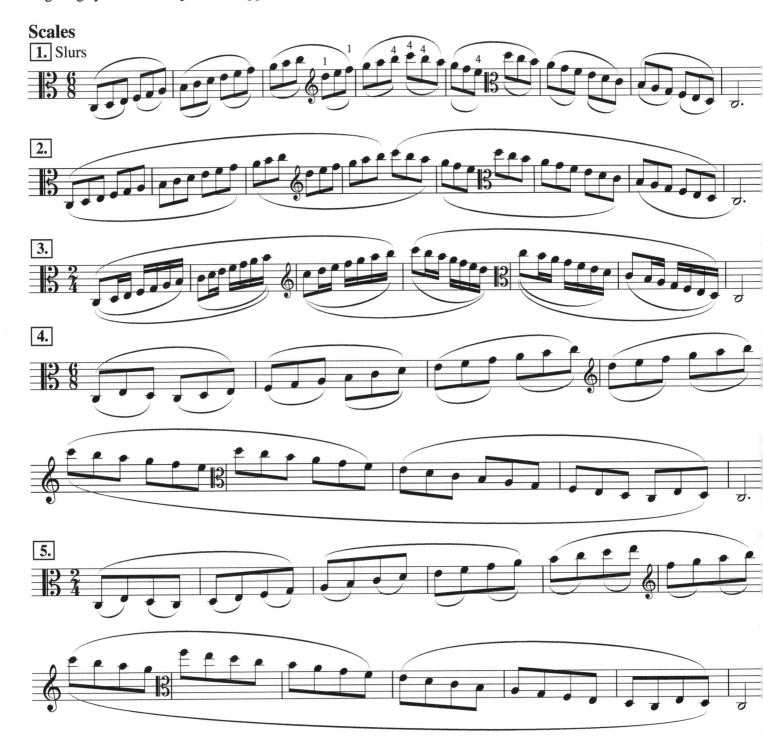

5. Left Hand Acceleration

Arpeggios

7. Forwards and Backwards - play with or without slurs

8. 3 + 1

4 + 1

6

9. Repeat top octave as needed

10. Slurs

11. L.H. velocity

Broken Thirds

12. Practice shifts forwards and backwards

13. Slurs

et

Chromatic

14. 4 + 1

15. Slurs

et

Bowings - Practice bowings with and without various rhythms.

Rhythms - Practice rhythms with and without various bowings.

Practice Suggestions for Double-Stops

When playing double-stops, the fingers used in the first double-stop remain on the string as anchors until the fingers for the next double-stop have been placed. This kind of "walking" finger action produces smooth, efficient motion in the left hand. It also aids the hand in estimating the correct combinations and distances of half-steps and whole-steps to ensure acurate intonation. When the same fingers move to a new double-stop by means of a shift, they are not lifted but rather glide on the strings from one position to the next.

The following introductory exercises for octaves and thirds are based on the concept of placing the fingers individually. On the *ascending* scale, the fingers are placed in *ascending* numerical order, i.e. 0, 1, 2, 3 or 1, 2, 3, 4. On the *descending* scale, the fingers are placed in *descending* numerical order, i.e. 4, 3, 2, 1, or 3, 2, 1, 0. *Fingers should remain anchored whenever possible.*

After this introduction, the student may wish to proceed to p. 11, No. 7

Thirds - practice each shift separately   ⌄ = half step   ⋁⋁ = whole step

After this introduction, the student may wish to proceed to p. 11, No. 78 in 3rds.

* Or:

76.

Sixths

77.

etc.

78. Use these practice ideas with all double-stops.

Key of C

Broken Thirds

Chromatic

Octaves

Thirds

Sixths

Harmonics

Key of D♭/C♯

Major

Melodic Minor

Harmonic Minor

Tonic Minor

Tonic Major

Sub-mediant

Sub-dominant Major

Sub-dominant Minor

Diminished 7th

Dominant 7th

Key of D

Key of E♭

Broken Thirds

Chromatic

Octaves

Thirds

Sixths

Harmonics

Key of E

Key of F

Broken Thirds

Chromatic

Octaves

Thirds

Sixths

Harmonics

Key of F♯

Broken Thirds

Chromatic

Octaves

Thirds

Sixths

Harmonics

Key of G

Broken Thirds

Chromatic

Octaves

Thirds

Sixths

Harmonics

Key of A♭/G♯

Key of A

32

Key of B♭

Key of B

35

With more than 40 years of performing and teaching experience, violinist and violist Barbara Barber joined the sales team at Robertson & Sons Violin Shop, one of the world's premier bowed string instrument dealers, in Albuquerque, NM in 2014. Barbara has concertized and presented master classes and pedagogy clinics across the United States, and in Canada, Mexico, El Salvador, Brazil, Peru, Colombia, Australia, New Zealand, Korea, Taiwan, Hong Kong, Japan, Italy, Ireland, Finland, Sweden and Bermuda. She received her Bachelor of Music and Master of Music in performance at Texas Tech University with additional studies at Interlochen Music Camp, Rocky Ridge Music Center, Accademia di Chigiana in Italy, Taos School of Music and Banff Centre. Barbara has held faculty appointments at Texas Tech University, Texas Christian University and the University of Colorado. She has been recognized for her many articles, presentations and roles on the advisory and editorial boards of the American Strings Teachers Association and the Suzuki Association of the Americas. Barbara's widely-used collections of books and CDs are published by Preludio Music Inc. and distributed worldwide by Alfred Music.